Designing and Developing Medical Devices: A Student's Journey in Manufacturing Engineering

Martin

Copyright © [2023]

Title: Designing and Developing Medical Devices: A Student's Journey in Manufacturing Engineering
Author's: Martin

All rights reserved. No part of this publication may be reproduced, stored in a retrieval system, or transmitted in any form or by any means, electronic, mechanical, photocopying, recording, or otherwise, without the prior written permission of the publisher or author, except in the case of brief quotations embodied in critical reviews and certain other non-commercial uses permitted by copyright law.

This book was printed and published by [Publisher's: **Martin**] in [2023]

ISBN:

TABLE OF CONTENT

Chapter 1: Introduction to Medical Device Manufacturing Engineering   07

Understanding the Role of Manufacturing Engineering in Medical Device Development

Overview of the Medical Device Manufacturing Industry

Importance of Manufacturing Engineering in Medical Device Safety and Quality

Chapter 2: Fundamentals of Medical Device Design   14

Conceptualization and Ideation of Medical Devices

Design Validation and Verification

Human Factors and Ergonomics in Medical Device Design

Chapter 3: Materials and Manufacturing Processes for Medical Devices   21

Selection of Materials for Medical Devices

Machining and Fabrication Techniques in Medical Device Manufacturing

Additive Manufacturing in Medical Device Production

Chapter 4: Regulatory Considerations in Medical Device Manufacturing   27

Overview of Medical Device Regulations and Standards

Quality Systems and Good Manufacturing Practices (GMP)

Risk Management in Medical Device Manufacturing

Chapter 5: Prototyping and Testing of Medical Devices   33

Rapid Prototyping Techniques for Medical Devices

Testing and Validation of Medical Device Prototypes

Usability Testing and User Feedback

Chapter 6: Manufacturing Process Optimization and Scale-up   39

Process Optimization for Efficiency and Cost-effectiveness

Scale-up Strategies for Medical Device Manufacturing

Lean Manufacturing Principles in Medical Device Production

Chapter 7: Quality Control and Assurance in Medical Device Manufacturing 46

Inspection and Testing of Medical Devices

Statistical Process Control in Medical Device Manufacturing

Non-Destructive Testing Techniques for Quality Assurance

Chapter 8: Packaging and Sterilization of Medical Devices 52

Packaging Considerations for Medical Devices

Sterilization Methods and Validation

Shelf Life and Packaging Integrity Testing

Chapter 9: Post-Market Surveillance and Risk Management 58

Overview of Post-Market Surveillance

Adverse Event Reporting and Corrective Actions

Risk Management in the Post-Market Phase

Chapter 10: Future Trends and Innovations in Medical Device Manufacturing 64

Advances in Biomaterials for Medical Devices

Integration of Artificial Intelligence and Internet of Things (IoT) in Medical Device Manufacturing

Personalized Medicine and Customized Medical Devices

Chapter 11: Career Opportunities and Professional Development in Medical Device Manufacturing Engineering 72

Job Roles and Responsibilities in Medical Device Manufacturing

Continuing Education and Professional Certifications

Networking and Industry Engagement for Career Advancement

Chapter 12: Conclusion and Reflections on the Student's Journey in Medical Device Manufacturing Engineering 79

Chapter 1: Introduction to Medical Device Manufacturing Engineering

Understanding the Role of Manufacturing Engineering in Medical Device Development

Manufacturing engineering plays a critical role in the development of medical devices, ensuring that these life-saving technologies are not only safe and effective but also cost-efficient and scalable. This subchapter aims to provide students studying manufacturing engineering with a comprehensive understanding of their role in the medical device development process.

The field of manufacturing engineering focuses on the design, development, and implementation of efficient manufacturing processes and systems. When it comes to medical device development, manufacturing engineers are responsible for translating the design concept into a tangible product that can be mass-produced.

One of the key responsibilities of manufacturing engineers is to optimize the manufacturing process to meet the specific requirements of medical device production. This involves selecting appropriate materials, designing efficient assembly lines, and ensuring that the manufacturing process adheres to regulatory standards such as Good Manufacturing Practices (GMP) and ISO 13485.

Manufacturing engineers also collaborate closely with design engineers to ensure that the product design is manufacturable. They provide valuable input during the design phase, offering insights into material selection, component sourcing, and production feasibility. By working together, manufacturing engineers and design engineers can create a product that not only meets the functional requirements but is also easy to manufacture.

Another crucial aspect of manufacturing engineering in medical device development is quality control. Manufacturing engineers are responsible for developing and implementing quality control processes to ensure that each device meets the highest standards of safety and effectiveness. This involves conducting thorough inspections, tests, and certifications throughout the manufacturing process.

Furthermore, manufacturing engineers play a vital role in ensuring cost-effectiveness and scalability of medical device production. They are responsible for identifying areas where costs can be reduced without compromising the quality of the product. They also develop strategies to scale up production to meet increasing demand while maintaining efficiency and quality.

In conclusion, manufacturing engineering is an essential discipline in the development of medical devices. Students studying manufacturing engineering need to understand the critical role they play in translating design concepts into safe, cost-effective, and scalable medical devices. By working closely with design engineers, adhering to regulatory standards, implementing quality control processes, and optimizing manufacturing processes, manufacturing engineers contribute significantly to the successful development of medical devices that improve the quality of healthcare.

Overview of the Medical Device Manufacturing Industry

In recent years, the medical device manufacturing industry has experienced significant growth, making it a compelling field for students pursuing a career in manufacturing engineering. This subchapter provides an overview of the industry, highlighting its importance, trends, and opportunities for students.

The medical device manufacturing industry plays a crucial role in the healthcare sector by producing a wide range of devices that aid in the diagnosis, treatment, and management of medical conditions. From simple instruments like thermometers and syringes to complex devices such as pacemakers and robotic surgical systems, these technologies have revolutionized healthcare and improved patient outcomes.

One of the main driving factors behind the growth of this industry is the increasing demand for innovative medical devices. Advancements in technology, coupled with an aging population and rising healthcare expenditure, have created a fertile ground for the development of new and improved medical devices. This has opened up numerous opportunities for students to contribute to the field through their expertise in manufacturing engineering.

In addition to the demand for innovation, the medical device manufacturing industry is also subject to stringent regulatory requirements. Governments and regulatory bodies around the world have implemented strict guidelines to ensure the safety and efficacy of medical devices. This creates a need for skilled professionals who can navigate complex regulatory landscapes and ensure compliance throughout the manufacturing process.

Moreover, the industry is witnessing a shift towards personalized medicine and the integration of digital technologies. Medical devices now incorporate features such as wireless connectivity, data analytics, and artificial intelligence, enabling healthcare providers to deliver more personalized and efficient care. As a result, students with a background in manufacturing engineering have an opportunity to contribute to the development of these technologies and help shape the future of healthcare.

To excel in the medical device manufacturing industry, students must acquire a diverse set of skills. Knowledge of manufacturing processes, materials, quality control, and regulatory compliance are essential. Additionally, students should be familiar with emerging technologies, such as additive manufacturing and robotics, which are transforming the way medical devices are designed and manufactured.

In conclusion, the medical device manufacturing industry presents exciting prospects for students in the field of manufacturing engineering. With the increasing demand for innovative devices, stringent regulatory requirements, and the integration of digital technologies, students have an opportunity to make a significant impact in improving healthcare outcomes. By acquiring the necessary skills and knowledge, students can embark on a rewarding journey in this dynamic and rapidly evolving industry.

Importance of Manufacturing Engineering in Medical Device Safety and Quality

The Importance of Manufacturing Engineering in Medical Device Safety and Quality

Introduction:

In the fast-paced world of healthcare, the development and manufacturing of medical devices play a critical role in saving lives and improving patient outcomes. Manufacturing engineering is a vital discipline that ensures the safety and quality of these devices. This subchapter will delve into the significance of manufacturing engineering in the context of medical device safety and quality, aimed specifically at students interested in pursuing a career in manufacturing engineering within the medical device industry.

Enhancing Safety:

Manufacturing engineering focuses on implementing stringent safety measures throughout the entire production process. Medical devices must comply with strict regulations and standards to ensure their safety and efficacy. By ensuring that devices are manufactured according to these standards, manufacturing engineers contribute to the reduction of potential risks and hazards for patients. Through their expertise, they can identify potential issues and develop strategies to mitigate them, leading to safer medical devices.

Ensuring Quality:

Manufacturing engineering is essential in maintaining the highest levels of quality in medical device production. By implementing quality control measures, such as statistical process control and rigorous testing procedures, manufacturing engineers ensure that each device meets the required specifications. This attention to detail and commitment to quality ensures that medical devices function as intended, providing accurate diagnostics and effective treatments.

Process Optimization:

Manufacturing engineering plays a vital role in optimizing the production process of medical devices. With advancements in technology, manufacturing engineers can identify areas for improvement and implement innovative manufacturing techniques. By streamlining processes, reducing waste, and improving efficiency, manufacturing engineers contribute to the timely and cost-effective production of medical devices without compromising safety or quality.

Regulatory Compliance:

The medical device industry is heavily regulated to safeguard patient health and well-being. Manufacturing engineers are responsible for ensuring compliance with these regulations. They work closely with regulatory bodies, such as the Food and Drug Administration (FDA), to understand and implement the necessary procedures. Students interested in manufacturing engineering must possess a strong understanding of regulations and stay updated with the latest developments to ensure compliance throughout the device's lifecycle.

Conclusion:

Manufacturing engineering is a critical discipline in the medical device industry, ensuring the safety and quality of devices that save lives and improve patient outcomes. This subchapter has highlighted the importance of manufacturing engineering in enhancing safety, ensuring quality, optimizing processes, and ensuring regulatory compliance within the medical device manufacturing process. As students interested in manufacturing engineering, understanding and embracing these concepts will lay a strong foundation for a successful career in the medical device industry, where their skills and expertise can make a profound impact on patient care.

Chapter 2: Fundamentals of Medical Device Design

Conceptualization and Ideation of Medical Devices

Introduction:
In the field of manufacturing engineering, the design and development of medical devices play a crucial role in improving healthcare and enhancing patient outcomes. This subchapter aims to provide students with a comprehensive understanding of the conceptualization and ideation process involved in creating innovative medical devices. By exploring the key stages and considerations in this process, students will gain valuable insights into the complex and rewarding world of medical device design.

Understanding the Medical Device Design Process: The conceptualization and ideation stage is the foundation of any successful medical device development project. It involves generating and refining ideas, as well as evaluating their feasibility and potential impact. Students will learn about the importance of understanding user needs and market dynamics, as well as conducting thorough research and analysis to identify opportunities for innovation.

Generating Ideas:
Brainstorming is a powerful technique for generating ideas during the conceptualization phase. Students will be introduced to various brainstorming methods, such as mind mapping and SCAMPER, which can help them think creatively and generate a wide range of ideas. They will also learn about the significance of interdisciplinary collaboration and how it can contribute to the ideation process.

Evaluating Feasibility:
Once a set of ideas has been generated, students will delve into evaluating the feasibility of each concept. They will learn about factors such as technical feasibility, regulatory requirements, manufacturing constraints, and cost considerations. Understanding these aspects will enable students to make informed decisions about the viability of their ideas and refine them accordingly.

Prototyping and Testing:
Prototyping and testing are essential steps in the ideation and conceptualization process. Students will explore different prototyping techniques, including 3D printing, and understand their role in bringing ideas to life. They will also learn about the importance of usability testing and obtaining feedback from end-users to refine their designs and ensure they meet the intended purpose.

Iterative Design Process:
Students will gain an understanding of the iterative nature of the design process and how it applies to medical device development. They will discover the value of continuous improvement and learn how to incorporate feedback into the design cycle to optimize their prototypes.

Conclusion:
Conceptualization and ideation are critical phases in the design and development of medical devices. By fostering a deep understanding of user needs, conducting thorough research, and employing creative thinking techniques, students can generate innovative ideas that have the potential to revolutionize healthcare. Through prototyping, testing, and iteration, they can refine their designs and contribute to

the manufacturing engineering field by developing medical devices that address real-world challenges and improve the lives of patients.

Design Validation and Verification

In the field of manufacturing engineering, the process of designing and developing medical devices requires meticulous attention to detail and rigorous testing to ensure their safety and effectiveness. This subchapter, titled "Design Validation and Verification," aims to provide students with a comprehensive understanding of the importance of validation and verification in the medical device industry.

Design validation is a crucial step in the development process, involving the evaluation of a product's performance under real-world conditions. It ensures that the device meets all the specified requirements, functions as intended, and performs reliably. Students will learn about the various methods used in design validation, such as simulated testing, usability studies, and clinical trials. They will also gain insights into the regulatory standards and guidelines that govern the validation process, ensuring compliance with industry regulations.

Verification, on the other hand, focuses on assessing whether the design outputs meet the specified design inputs. It involves thorough testing, inspection, and analysis to ensure that the design meets all the predetermined requirements. Through this subchapter, students will gain an understanding of the verification process, including the use of testing equipment, statistical analysis, and documentation. They will also learn about the importance of traceability, as verification activities need to be thoroughly documented to ensure accountability and transparency.

Furthermore, this subchapter will delve into the challenges and considerations specific to medical device design validation and verification. Students will explore the impact of design changes, risk management, and the importance of collaboration between engineering teams and other stakeholders. They will also learn about the role of human factors engineering in the validation and verification process, emphasizing the need for user-centered design to ensure the safety and usability of medical devices.

Through case studies and practical examples, students will gain a hands-on understanding of the design validation and verification process. They will be introduced to the tools and techniques used in testing, data analysis, and reporting. Moreover, this subchapter will highlight the impact of validation and verification on the overall manufacturing process and the significance of continuous improvement to enhance product quality.

By the end of this subchapter, students will have a comprehensive knowledge of design validation and verification, equipping them with the skills necessary to ensure the development of safe and effective medical devices. They will understand the critical role of validation and verification in manufacturing engineering and be ready to contribute to the advancement of the medical device industry.

Human Factors and Ergonomics in Medical Device Design

In the fast-paced world of healthcare, medical devices play a crucial role in improving patient outcomes and enhancing the overall quality of care. However, the effectiveness and safety of these devices heavily rely on their design and usability. This subchapter explores the significance of human factors and ergonomics in the design of medical devices, with a focus on the manufacturing engineering niche.

Human factors refer to the study of how humans interact with systems, products, and environments. When it comes to medical device design, understanding the capabilities and limitations of human users is of paramount importance. From the initial conceptualization to the final product, every step of the design process must consider the end-users – the healthcare professionals and patients. By integrating human factors into the design, medical devices can be optimized for efficiency, safety, and user satisfaction.

Ergonomics, on the other hand, focuses on designing devices that fit the human body and its movements. In the context of medical devices, ergonomics ensures that the equipment is comfortable, easy to handle, and minimizes the risk of musculoskeletal disorders for healthcare professionals. By considering factors such as body posture, hand movements, and cognitive workload, medical device designers can create products that facilitate seamless interactions between the user and the device.

This subchapter delves into the various considerations and challenges faced by manufacturing engineering students when incorporating human factors and ergonomics in medical device design. It explores the importance of user-centered design principles, such as conducting usability testing and gathering feedback from potential users throughout the design process. It also highlights the significance of integrating human factors and ergonomics into the risk management and regulatory frameworks associated with medical device development.

Furthermore, this subchapter provides practical insights into the implementation of human factors and ergonomics in manufacturing engineering, including the use of 3D modeling and simulation tools to optimize device design. It also discusses the importance of interdisciplinary collaboration between manufacturing engineers, healthcare professionals, and human factors specialists to ensure that medical devices meet the needs of both users and manufacturers.

By understanding and incorporating human factors and ergonomics in medical device design, manufacturing engineering students can contribute to the development of innovative and user-friendly devices that improve patient outcomes and enhance the overall healthcare experience. This subchapter serves as a comprehensive guide for students interested in the intersection of manufacturing engineering, human factors, and medical device design, providing them with the necessary knowledge and tools to excel in this dynamic field.

Chapter 3: Materials and Manufacturing Processes for Medical Devices

Selection of Materials for Medical Devices

In the field of manufacturing engineering, the development of medical devices holds immense importance. These devices play a crucial role in improving the quality of healthcare and saving lives. However, designing and developing medical devices is a complex and challenging process that requires meticulous attention to detail, especially when it comes to selecting the right materials.

The selection of materials for medical devices is a critical step that directly impacts the device's performance, safety, and longevity. The chosen materials must meet stringent requirements, including biocompatibility, durability, sterilizability, and ease of manufacturing. It is essential for students in the field of manufacturing engineering to understand the factors influencing material selection and make informed decisions to ensure the success of their medical device projects.

Biocompatibility is one of the primary considerations in material selection. Medical devices come into direct contact with the human body, and any adverse reaction can have severe consequences. Students must understand the biocompatibility testing protocols and choose materials that are non-toxic, non-allergenic, and compatible with human tissues and fluids.

Durability is another crucial aspect to consider. Medical devices are subjected to various mechanical forces, temperature fluctuations, and exposure to chemicals. Students need to select materials with sufficient strength, wear resistance, and corrosion resistance to withstand these conditions and ensure the device's long-term reliability.

Sterilizability is also a key factor to keep in mind. Medical devices must undergo sterilization processes to eliminate harmful microorganisms. Students should consider materials that can withstand the chosen sterilization method without compromising their properties or functionality.

Ease of manufacturing is an often overlooked aspect of material selection. Students need to choose materials that can be easily machined, molded, or fabricated into the desired shape. The manufacturing process should be efficient, cost-effective, and scalable to meet the demands of mass production.

Moreover, students should explore the latest advancements in materials science, such as biodegradable polymers, shape memory alloys, and nanomaterials. These innovative materials offer unique properties and functionalities that can revolutionize the design and performance of medical devices.

In conclusion, the selection of materials for medical devices is a critical step in the manufacturing engineering process. Students must consider factors such as biocompatibility, durability, sterilizability, and ease of manufacturing to ensure the success and safety of their projects. By staying updated with the latest advancements in materials science, students can push the boundaries of medical device design and contribute to the advancement of healthcare technology.

Machining and Fabrication Techniques in Medical Device Manufacturing

In the field of manufacturing engineering, the production of medical devices requires specialized techniques to ensure the highest quality and precision. This subchapter aims to provide students with an insight into the various machining and fabrication techniques used in the manufacturing of medical devices.

Machining, which involves removing material from a workpiece to create the desired shape and size, plays a crucial role in medical device manufacturing. One commonly used technique is computer numerical control (CNC) machining. CNC machines utilize computer programming to control the movement of cutting tools, resulting in highly accurate and repeatable manufacturing processes. Students will learn about the different CNC machining methods such as milling, turning, and drilling, and how these techniques are applied in the production of medical devices.

Another important aspect of medical device manufacturing is fabrication, which involves joining multiple components together to create a functional device. Welding is a widely used fabrication technique that students will explore in this subchapter. They will gain an understanding of different welding processes such as laser welding, resistance welding, and ultrasonic welding, and how these techniques are employed to ensure strong and reliable joints in medical devices.

Additionally, the subchapter will cover additive manufacturing, also known as 3D printing, which has revolutionized the production of medical devices. Students will learn about the different types of 3D printing technologies and materials used, as well as the advantages and limitations of this technique in medical device manufacturing. They will gain insights into how 3D printing enables the rapid prototyping of medical devices, customization for patient-specific applications, and the production of complex geometries that would be challenging to achieve with traditional manufacturing methods.

Throughout this subchapter, students will be encouraged to consider the unique challenges and requirements of medical device manufacturing, such as the need for biocompatible materials, sterile manufacturing environments, and adherence to strict regulatory standards. By understanding the machining and fabrication techniques employed in this field, students will be equipped with the knowledge and skills necessary to contribute to the development of innovative medical devices that improve patient outcomes and enhance healthcare delivery.

In conclusion, "Machining and Fabrication Techniques in Medical Device Manufacturing" is a subchapter that provides students specializing in manufacturing engineering with an overview of the essential techniques used in the production of medical devices. This subchapter aims to enhance their understanding of CNC machining, fabrication, and additive manufacturing, while emphasizing the unique requirements and challenges associated with medical device manufacturing. By gaining insights into these techniques, students will be well-prepared to contribute to the advancement of medical device technology and make a positive impact on the healthcare industry.

Additive Manufacturing in Medical Device Production

In recent years, additive manufacturing, also known as 3D printing, has emerged as a revolutionary technology in the field of manufacturing engineering. This groundbreaking process has found numerous applications in various industries, and one of the most promising areas where it has made significant advancements is in medical device production.

The medical device industry plays a crucial role in improving patient outcomes and enhancing the quality of healthcare. However, traditional manufacturing methods for medical devices often involve complex and time-consuming processes, which can lead to increased costs and longer lead times. Additive manufacturing has the potential to address these challenges by providing a more efficient and cost-effective solution.

One of the key advantages of additive manufacturing in medical device production is its ability to create highly customized and patient-specific devices. By utilizing digital design files, medical professionals and engineers can tailor implants, prosthetics, and surgical instruments to match the specific needs of individual patients. This level of customization not only improves the effectiveness of the devices but also enhances patient comfort and overall satisfaction.

Moreover, additive manufacturing allows for the production of complex geometries and intricate structures that would be difficult or even impossible to achieve using traditional manufacturing methods. This capability opens up new possibilities for the creation of innovative medical devices with improved functionality and performance. For example, 3D printing has been used to produce implantable devices with porous structures that promote bone ingrowth, leading to better integration and long-term success rates.

In addition to its customization and complex design capabilities, additive manufacturing also offers the potential for cost savings and reduced production times. By eliminating the need for tooling and reducing material waste, this technology can streamline the manufacturing process, resulting in shorter lead times and lower production costs. This is particularly beneficial in the healthcare industry, where quick delivery and cost efficiency are of utmost importance.

However, it is important to note that additive manufacturing in medical device production also poses challenges and considerations. Quality control, material selection, and regulatory compliance are critical factors that must be carefully managed to ensure the safety and efficacy of the produced devices.

In conclusion, additive manufacturing has emerged as a game-changer in the field of medical device production. Its ability to create customized devices, produce complex geometries, and streamline the manufacturing process offers immense potential for improving patient outcomes and advancing the healthcare industry. As students in the field of manufacturing engineering, it is crucial to stay updated with the latest advancements in additive manufacturing and leverage this technology to drive innovation in medical device production.

Chapter 4: Regulatory Considerations in Medical Device Manufacturing

Overview of Medical Device Regulations and Standards

In the fast-paced world of medical device manufacturing, it is crucial for students pursuing a career in manufacturing engineering to understand the regulations and standards that govern the design and development of medical devices. This subchapter provides an overview of the key aspects of medical device regulations and standards, equipping students with the knowledge necessary to navigate this highly regulated industry.

Medical devices play a critical role in patient care, ranging from simple tools like thermometers to complex devices such as pacemakers. Due to the potential risks associated with these devices, regulatory bodies have established stringent guidelines to ensure their safety, efficacy, and quality. The subchapter delves into the major regulatory bodies and standards, including the Food and Drug Administration (FDA) in the United States, the European Medicines Agency (EMA) in Europe, and the International Organization for Standardization (ISO) worldwide.

The FDA, as one of the most influential regulatory bodies, sets the standards for medical device manufacturers in the US. Students will gain insights into the FDA's classification system for medical devices, which categorizes devices based on their potential risks to patients. The subchapter also explores the FDA's premarket approval process, which involves rigorous testing and documentation requirements to ensure the safety and effectiveness of medical devices before they can be marketed.

In the European Union, the EMA oversees the regulation of medical devices through the Medical Device Regulation (MDR). Students will learn about the MDR's essential requirements and conformity assessment procedures, which must be met by manufacturers to obtain the CE marking, indicating compliance with EU regulations.

Additionally, the subchapter provides an overview of ISO standards, which are globally recognized and widely adopted by medical device manufacturers. ISO standards such as ISO 13485 outline the requirements for a quality management system specific to the design, development, and production of medical devices. Students will understand the importance of adhering to ISO standards to ensure the safety and reliability of their products.

By understanding the regulations and standards in the medical device industry, students will be well-equipped to design and develop medical devices that comply with the necessary requirements. This subchapter serves as a foundation for further exploration into the intricacies of medical device regulations, empowering students to make informed decisions and contribute to the advancement of manufacturing engineering in the healthcare sector.

Quality Systems and Good Manufacturing Practices (GMP)

In the field of Manufacturing Engineering, the importance of quality systems and good manufacturing practices (GMP) cannot be overstated. These are essential components in the design and development of medical devices, ensuring that they meet the highest standards of safety, effectiveness, and reliability.

Quality systems encompass a set of procedures and processes that are put in place to ensure that the medical devices being manufactured are of superior quality. These systems are designed to identify potential issues or defects early on in the manufacturing process, allowing for timely corrective actions to be taken. By implementing a robust quality system, manufacturers can minimize the risks associated with product failures, reduce costs associated with rework or recalls, and enhance customer satisfaction.

One of the key aspects of quality systems is compliance with Good Manufacturing Practices (GMP). GMP is a set of guidelines and regulations that define the minimum requirements for the manufacturing, packaging, and labeling of medical devices. These practices ensure that the devices are consistently produced and controlled according to established quality standards.

GMP covers various aspects of the manufacturing process, including facility design, equipment calibration and maintenance, personnel training, documentation, and record-keeping. Adhering to GMP guidelines is crucial for manufacturers as it helps to ensure product safety, efficacy, and traceability. It also provides a framework for continuous improvement, enabling manufacturers to constantly evaluate and enhance their manufacturing processes.

For students pursuing a career in Manufacturing Engineering, understanding quality systems and GMP is essential. As future professionals in the medical device industry, they will be responsible for designing, developing, and manufacturing devices that are critical to patient health and well-being. By familiarizing themselves with quality systems and GMP, students can gain the necessary knowledge and skills to ensure that the devices they create are of the highest quality.

Moreover, students will also learn about the regulatory requirements associated with quality systems and GMP. They will become familiar with organizations such as the Food and Drug Administration (FDA) and the International Organization for Standardization (ISO), which play a crucial role in setting and enforcing standards for medical device manufacturing.

In conclusion, quality systems and Good Manufacturing Practices are vital in the field of Manufacturing Engineering, particularly in the design and development of medical devices. Students pursuing a career in this niche must understand the importance of these practices and the regulatory framework surrounding them. By incorporating quality systems and GMP into their education and future work, students can contribute to the production of safe, effective, and reliable medical devices that improve patient outcomes.

Risk Management in Medical Device Manufacturing

Risk management is a crucial aspect of the manufacturing process in the medical device industry. It involves identifying, evaluating, and mitigating potential risks to ensure the safety and effectiveness of the medical devices being produced. As students in the field of manufacturing engineering, understanding and implementing risk management strategies is vital to your future career in the medical device industry.

The first step in risk management is to identify potential risks. This can be done through a comprehensive analysis of the manufacturing process, including all the stages involved in the production of a medical device. Risks can arise from various factors, such as design flaws, manufacturing errors, inadequate quality control, or improper use of materials. By identifying these risks early on, you can develop strategies to address them before they become significant issues.

Once the risks have been identified, the next step is to evaluate their potential impact on the safety and effectiveness of the medical device. This involves assessing the severity of the risks and the likelihood of their occurrence. By assigning a risk level to each identified risk, you can prioritize them and focus on mitigating the most critical ones first.

Mitigating risks involves implementing strategies to reduce or eliminate the likelihood and impact of potential risks. This can include implementing quality control measures, conducting thorough testing and validation procedures, and ensuring compliance with regulatory requirements. It is essential to establish clear protocols and guidelines for all manufacturing processes to minimize the occurrence of errors and ensure consistent quality.

Regular monitoring and evaluation of the manufacturing process are also crucial to risk management. This involves ongoing inspections and audits to identify any deviations or potential risks that may have arisen during the production process. By continuously monitoring and evaluating the manufacturing process, you can take corrective actions promptly and prevent any potential risks from compromising the safety and effectiveness of the medical devices.

In conclusion, risk management plays a vital role in medical device manufacturing. As students in the field of manufacturing engineering, it is crucial to understand the importance of identifying, evaluating, and mitigating risks to ensure the safety and effectiveness of medical devices. By implementing robust risk management strategies, you can contribute to the development of high-quality and reliable medical devices that meet regulatory standards and improve patient care.

Chapter 5: Prototyping and Testing of Medical Devices

Rapid Prototyping Techniques for Medical Devices

In the field of manufacturing engineering, the development of medical devices poses unique challenges due to the stringent requirements of the healthcare industry. The ability to rapidly prototype and iterate on designs is crucial for ensuring the safety and effectiveness of these life-saving devices. This subchapter will explore various rapid prototyping techniques that students in the field of manufacturing engineering can utilize to enhance the design and development process of medical devices.

One of the most widely used rapid prototyping techniques in the medical device industry is 3D printing. This additive manufacturing process allows for the creation of complex geometries and intricate features that are often required in medical devices. Students can leverage 3D printing technologies to quickly produce prototypes of medical devices, enabling them to test and refine their designs before moving to expensive and time-consuming manufacturing processes.

Another valuable rapid prototyping technique is computer numerical control (CNC) machining. CNC machines use pre-programmed computer software to control the movement of tools and create precise parts from various materials. This technique is particularly useful for producing functional prototypes of medical devices with high accuracy and intricate details. By utilizing CNC machining, students can create prototypes that closely resemble the final product, facilitating further testing and evaluation.

Additionally, this subchapter will introduce students to the concept of rapid prototyping using soft materials such as silicone and polyurethane. These materials allow for the creation of flexible prototypes, ideal for simulating the behavior of human tissues and organs. Students will learn how to use soft materials to develop realistic models for testing and validation purposes, enabling them to better understand the performance and functionality of their medical device designs.

Furthermore, this subchapter will delve into the utilization of rapid prototyping techniques in the context of regulatory compliance. Students will gain insight into the importance of adhering to strict regulations and standards when developing medical devices. By utilizing rapid prototyping techniques, students can iterate on their designs more efficiently, ensuring that their final products meet the necessary regulatory requirements.

In conclusion, rapid prototyping techniques play a vital role in the design and development of medical devices. This subchapter has provided an overview of various rapid prototyping techniques, such as 3D printing, CNC machining, and soft material prototyping. By implementing these techniques, students in the field of manufacturing engineering can enhance their ability to innovate and create safe and effective medical devices.

Testing and Validation of Medical Device Prototypes

In the realm of manufacturing engineering, the development and production of medical devices require utmost precision and accuracy to ensure the safety and efficacy of these devices. This subchapter aims to shed light on the crucial process of testing and validating medical device prototypes, providing valuable insights and practical tips for students in the field of manufacturing engineering.

The process of testing and validating medical device prototypes is an essential step in bringing a new product to market. It involves rigorous assessments to ensure that the device meets the required standards and specifications, as well as regulatory compliance. This phase not only evaluates the performance and functionality of the prototype but also identifies any potential design flaws or areas for improvement.

One of the primary objectives of testing and validation is to determine the device's ability to perform its intended function accurately and consistently. This involves conducting various tests, such as mechanical, electrical, and performance tests, to assess the device's durability, reliability, and overall functionality. Students need to understand the importance of following standardized testing procedures and protocols to obtain reliable and reproducible results.

Furthermore, validation is crucial to ensure that the medical device is safe and effective for use by healthcare professionals and patients. This entails conducting biocompatibility testing to assess the device's compatibility with living tissues and fluids, as well as sterilization validation to ensure that the device can be effectively cleaned and sterilized without compromising its performance.

In addition to testing the device itself, it is equally important to evaluate the manufacturing process and quality control measures. This includes conducting process validation to ensure that the manufacturing process consistently produces devices that meet the required specifications. By implementing robust quality control measures, students can ensure that each device produced is of high quality and free from defects.

To successfully test and validate medical device prototypes, students should familiarize themselves with relevant industry standards, regulatory requirements, and testing methodologies. They should also learn to interpret and analyze test results accurately, as this information will guide further design iterations and improvements.

In conclusion, testing and validating medical device prototypes is a critical step in the manufacturing engineering journey. It ensures that the devices meet the necessary standards, function as intended, and are safe for use. By understanding the importance of testing and validation, students can contribute to the development of innovative and reliable medical devices that improve patient outcomes and revolutionize healthcare practices.

Usability Testing and User Feedback

As students in the field of manufacturing engineering, it is essential to understand the critical role of usability testing and user feedback in the design and development of medical devices. In this subchapter, we will explore the importance of involving the end-users in the design process and how their feedback can significantly impact the success of a medical device.

Usability testing is a systematic evaluation method used to assess the ease of use, efficiency, and overall user experience of a product. In the context of medical devices, it involves observing real users as they interact with the device to identify any usability issues and gather feedback for improvements. This testing phase is crucial as it ensures that the device meets the needs of the intended users, promotes user satisfaction, and minimizes the risk of errors or accidents.

To conduct usability testing effectively, it is essential to define clear objectives and develop realistic scenarios that simulate real-life situations. This allows users to perform tasks that are relevant to their daily lives, providing valuable insights into the device's usability. By observing users' interactions, collecting data, and recording their feedback, we can identify any design flaws, areas of improvement, or potential safety concerns early in the development process.

In addition to usability testing, gathering user feedback is crucial for refining the design and functionality of medical devices. Feedback can be obtained through various methods, such as surveys, interviews, focus groups, or online platforms. This feedback allows us to understand users' preferences, expectations, and challenges they may encounter while using the device. By actively involving users in the design process, we can ensure that the final product aligns with their needs and requirements, ultimately increasing its acceptance and adoption in the medical field.

Furthermore, user feedback also plays a vital role in regulatory compliance. Regulatory bodies, such as the Food and Drug Administration (FDA), emphasize the importance of human factors engineering and user feedback in the approval process of medical devices. Demonstrating that usability testing and user feedback were incorporated throughout the development process enhances the device's safety and effectiveness, thus expediting the regulatory approval.

In conclusion, usability testing and user feedback are integral components of the design and development of medical devices. As students in the field of manufacturing engineering, understanding the significance of involving end-users and gathering their feedback is essential for creating innovative and user-friendly medical devices. By prioritizing usability testing and user feedback, we can ensure that our designs meet the needs of patients and healthcare professionals while complying with regulatory standards.

Chapter 6: Manufacturing Process Optimization and Scale-up

Process Optimization for Efficiency and Cost-effectiveness

In the field of manufacturing engineering, process optimization plays a crucial role in ensuring the efficient and cost-effective production of medical devices. This subchapter will delve into the importance of process optimization and provide students with valuable insights on how to achieve it in the context of medical device manufacturing.

Efficiency is a key factor that directly impacts the success of any manufacturing process. By optimizing the production process, students can minimize waste, reduce cycle times, and increase productivity. This subchapter will explore various techniques and methodologies to achieve efficiency in medical device manufacturing.

One approach to process optimization is through the implementation of Lean Manufacturing principles. Students will learn how to identify and eliminate non-value-added activities, streamline workflows, and improve overall efficiency. Additionally, the concept of Six Sigma will be introduced, focusing on reducing process variations and defects to enhance quality and efficiency.

Cost-effectiveness is another critical aspect of process optimization. Manufacturing medical devices can be an expensive endeavor, and students must learn to identify cost drivers and implement strategies to minimize expenses. This subchapter will discuss cost optimization techniques such as value engineering, where the focus is on maximizing the value of the product while minimizing costs.

Furthermore, students will gain insights into the role of automation and advanced technologies in process optimization. From robotics and artificial intelligence to data analytics and machine learning, these innovative tools can greatly enhance efficiency and cost-effectiveness in medical device manufacturing. Case studies and real-world examples will be provided to illustrate the practical applications of these technologies.

Lastly, this subchapter will emphasize the importance of continuous improvement in process optimization. Students will be introduced to the concept of Kaizen, which promotes a culture of ongoing improvement. By constantly evaluating and refining processes, students can ensure that their manufacturing operations remain efficient and cost-effective in the long run.

In conclusion, process optimization is vital in the field of manufacturing engineering, especially in the context of medical device manufacturing. By achieving efficiency and cost-effectiveness, students can contribute to the development of high-quality, affordable medical devices. This subchapter will equip students with the necessary knowledge and tools to optimize processes and drive innovation in the manufacturing engineering niche.

Scale-up Strategies for Medical Device Manufacturing

In the field of manufacturing engineering, scaling up a medical device production process is a critical task that requires careful planning and execution. As students aspiring to become professionals in this niche, understanding the essential strategies for scaling up medical device manufacturing is vital for success in the industry.

1. Process Optimization: Before scaling up production, it is essential to optimize the manufacturing process to ensure efficiency and quality. This involves identifying and eliminating any bottlenecks, streamlining workflows, and conducting thorough process validations. By optimizing the manufacturing process, students can ensure that the final product meets regulatory requirements and customer expectations.

2. Capacity Planning: One of the challenges in scaling up medical device manufacturing is determining the required production capacity. Students need to understand the demand forecast and market trends to estimate the necessary equipment, manpower, and resources. It is crucial to strike a balance between meeting market demand and avoiding overcapacity, which can lead to financial losses.

3. Supplier Management: As the scale of production increases, students must develop effective supplier management strategies. This includes sourcing reliable suppliers who can provide high-quality materials, components, and equipment at competitive prices. Building strong relationships with

suppliers and having backup options is essential to ensure a steady supply chain during the scaling-up process.

4. Automation and Technology Integration: Integrating automation and advanced technologies into the manufacturing process can significantly improve efficiency and productivity. Students should explore the latest innovations in robotics, artificial intelligence, and data analytics to streamline operations and reduce human error. Automating repetitive tasks can free up human resources for more complex and critical activities.

5. Regulatory Compliance: Scaling up medical device manufacturing requires adherence to strict regulatory standards. Students need to familiarize themselves with the applicable regulations, such as Good Manufacturing Practices (GMP) and ISO 13485. Implementing robust quality control systems and documentation procedures is crucial to ensure compliance and maintain product safety and efficacy.

6. Continuous Improvement: Lastly, students should embrace a culture of continuous improvement in the manufacturing process. Implementing Lean Six Sigma principles, conducting regular audits, and soliciting feedback from customers and employees can help identify areas for enhancement. By continuously improving processes, students can optimize production efficiency, reduce costs, and enhance product quality.

In conclusion, scaling up medical device manufacturing is a complex task that requires careful planning and implementation. By understanding and implementing these scale-up strategies, students specializing in manufacturing engineering can effectively navigate the challenges and opportunities in the industry. Through process optimization, capacity planning, supplier management, automation, regulatory compliance, and continuous improvement, students can contribute to the successful scaling up of medical device manufacturing processes.

Lean Manufacturing Principles in Medical Device Production

In the fast-paced world of medical device production, efficiency and quality are of utmost importance. To meet the ever-increasing demand for these life-saving devices, manufacturers must adopt lean manufacturing principles. This subchapter will delve into the key principles of lean manufacturing and discuss their relevance in the medical device production industry.

Lean manufacturing is a systematic approach that aims to eliminate waste and optimize the production process. By implementing lean principles, manufacturers can achieve higher productivity, reduced costs, improved quality, and enhanced customer satisfaction. These principles can be effectively applied in the field of manufacturing engineering, especially in the production of medical devices.

The first principle of lean manufacturing is to identify and eliminate any form of waste. In medical device production, waste can manifest in various ways, such as excessive inventory, overproduction, defects, and unnecessary motion. By streamlining processes and eliminating waste, manufacturers can save time, reduce costs, and improve overall efficiency.

Another important principle is continuous improvement. In the medical device industry, technology and regulations are constantly evolving. Manufacturers must strive for continuous improvement to stay ahead of the competition and meet regulatory requirements. This involves regularly reviewing and refining processes, incorporating feedback from customers and employees, and embracing new technologies and techniques.

Standardization is another key principle in lean manufacturing. By standardizing processes and components, manufacturers can reduce variability and improve efficiency. This is particularly crucial in the medical device industry, where consistency and precision are paramount.

Just-in-time (JIT) manufacturing is another principle that can greatly benefit medical device production. JIT aims to produce and deliver products at the exact time they are needed, minimizing inventory and reducing the risk of obsolescence. This principle ensures that manufacturers have the right materials and components on hand without excess storage, saving costs and improving efficiency.

Finally, employee empowerment and engagement play a vital role in lean manufacturing. Manufacturers should encourage their workforce to actively contribute ideas for process improvement and provide them with the necessary training and resources. Engaged employees are more likely to identify and solve problems, resulting in a more efficient and innovative production process.

In conclusion, lean manufacturing principles offer valuable insights for students of manufacturing engineering in the medical device production industry. By adopting these principles, manufacturers can improve productivity, reduce costs, enhance quality, and ultimately deliver life-saving devices to those in need.

Chapter 7: Quality Control and Assurance in Medical Device Manufacturing

Inspection and Testing of Medical Devices

In the field of manufacturing engineering, the inspection and testing of medical devices play a crucial role in ensuring the safety, efficacy, and reliability of these life-saving products. This subchapter aims to provide students with a comprehensive understanding of the various inspection and testing techniques used in the manufacturing of medical devices.

The inspection process involves examining the physical characteristics, dimensions, and functionality of medical devices to ensure they meet the design specifications and regulatory standards. This includes visual inspections, dimensional measurements, and functional testing. Visual inspections are performed to identify any defects, surface irregularities, or inconsistencies in the appearance of the device. Dimensional measurements are carried out using precise tools and instruments to verify that the device meets the required specifications. Functional testing is conducted to assess the device's performance under real-life conditions and to ensure it functions as intended.

In addition to traditional inspection methods, advanced technologies such as computer-aided inspection systems, non-destructive testing, and automated inspection systems are being increasingly employed in the manufacturing of medical devices. These technologies enhance the accuracy, efficiency, and reliability of the inspection process. Students will learn about these cutting-edge technologies and their application in the medical device industry.

Furthermore, this subchapter will delve into the regulatory requirements governing the inspection and testing of medical devices. Students will gain knowledge about the various international standards and regulations, such as ISO 13485 and FDA guidelines, which govern the quality management systems and testing protocols for medical devices. Understanding these regulations is crucial for ensuring compliance and meeting the stringent quality requirements in the manufacturing of medical devices.

Lastly, this subchapter will emphasize the importance of documentation and traceability in the inspection and testing process. Students will learn about the significance of maintaining accurate records of inspection results, testing procedures, and equipment calibration. Documentation plays a critical role in ensuring product quality, facilitating audits, and tracking any issues that may arise during the inspection and testing process.

By studying this subchapter on the inspection and testing of medical devices, students will gain a comprehensive understanding of the essential techniques, technologies, regulations, and documentation procedures that are vital in the manufacturing engineering field. This knowledge will equip them with the necessary skills to contribute to the design, development, and manufacturing of safe and effective medical devices.

Statistical Process Control in Medical Device Manufacturing

Statistical Process Control (SPC) plays a crucial role in ensuring the quality and reliability of medical devices during the manufacturing process. In this subchapter, we will explore the significance of SPC in medical device manufacturing and delve into its key principles and implementation strategies.

SPC is a statistical method used to monitor and control the manufacturing process, enabling manufacturers to identify and address potential variations or defects early on. This is particularly important in the medical device industry, where even minor errors or deviations can have severe consequences on patient safety and well-being.

One of the key principles of SPC is the concept of variation. Variations can occur due to various factors such as raw material quality, machine performance, or human error. SPC helps in understanding and managing these variations by collecting and analyzing data throughout the manufacturing process. By utilizing statistical tools like control charts, histograms, and process capability indices, manufacturers can identify trends, patterns, and anomalies in the data, allowing them to take proactive measures to maintain the desired quality standards.

Implementing SPC in medical device manufacturing involves several steps. Firstly, it requires the establishment of a robust data collection system to gather process-related data at regular intervals. This data can include measurements of critical parameters, such as dimensional accuracy, material strength, or electrical properties, depending on the type of medical device being manufactured.

Once the data is collected, it is analyzed using statistical techniques to identify any deviations from the desired specifications. Control charts are commonly used to visualize the data and determine whether the process is in control or experiencing any special cause variation. If any anomalies are detected, appropriate corrective actions can be taken to rectify the issue and bring the process back to a stable state.

SPC also emphasizes the importance of ongoing process monitoring and continuous improvement. By regularly analyzing data and updating control limits, manufacturers can ensure that the manufacturing process remains stable and consistent over time. This not only enhances product quality but also reduces the likelihood of product recalls or adverse events.

In conclusion, Statistical Process Control is a vital tool in the field of medical device manufacturing. By implementing SPC techniques, students in the field of Manufacturing Engineering can gain a deeper understanding of the importance of data analysis and statistical methods in ensuring the quality and reliability of medical devices. SPC enables manufacturers to detect and address process variations, leading to enhanced patient safety and improved overall product quality.

Non-Destructive Testing Techniques for Quality Assurance

Quality assurance is crucial in the field of manufacturing engineering, especially when it comes to designing and developing medical devices. Ensuring the safety and functionality of these devices is of utmost importance, and non-destructive testing (NDT) techniques play a vital role in achieving these goals.

Non-destructive testing refers to a range of inspection methods that allow for the evaluation of materials and components without causing any damage. These techniques are particularly valuable in the medical device industry, where the integrity and reliability of the products can directly impact patient health and well-being.

One commonly used NDT technique in quality assurance is visual inspection. This involves carefully examining the device for any visible defects, such as cracks, scratches, or irregularities in shape or surface finish. Visual inspection is a simple yet effective method to quickly identify any obvious flaws that may affect the device's performance.

Another widely employed NDT technique is ultrasonic testing. This method uses high-frequency sound waves to detect internal defects or irregularities within a material or component. By analyzing the reflected sound waves, manufacturing engineers can identify discontinuities, such as voids, delaminations, or inclusions, that may compromise the device's structural integrity.

Radiographic testing is yet another valuable NDT technique for quality assurance in medical device manufacturing. This method involves exposing the device to X-rays or gamma rays and capturing the resulting image on a radiographic film or digital detector. This allows for the detection of internal flaws, such as fractures, porosity, or foreign objects, which may not be visible to the naked eye.

Furthermore, magnetic particle testing is a highly effective NDT technique for detecting surface and near-surface defects. By applying a magnetic field to the device and using iron particles, any discontinuities that interrupt the magnetic field lines can be easily detected. This method is particularly useful for ferromagnetic materials commonly used in medical device manufacturing.

In conclusion, non-destructive testing techniques are essential tools in ensuring the quality of medical devices in the field of manufacturing engineering. Visual inspection, ultrasonic testing, radiographic testing, and magnetic particle testing are just a few examples of the numerous NDT techniques available. By employing these methods, manufacturing engineers can identify and rectify any flaws or defects, ultimately enhancing the safety and reliability of medical devices. As students pursuing a career in manufacturing engineering, it is crucial to understand and master these NDT techniques to contribute effectively to the development and manufacturing of high-quality medical devices.

Chapter 8: Packaging and Sterilization of Medical Devices

Packaging Considerations for Medical Devices

In the field of manufacturing engineering, the design and development of medical devices are critical tasks that require careful attention to every detail. One crucial aspect that often goes unnoticed is the packaging of these devices. Packaging plays a vital role in ensuring the safety and efficacy of medical devices, as well as their protection during transportation and storage. This subchapter aims to shed light on the important considerations that students in the field of manufacturing engineering need to keep in mind when it comes to packaging medical devices.

First and foremost, regulatory compliance should be the top priority. Medical devices are subject to stringent regulations and standards, such as those set by the Food and Drug Administration (FDA) in the United States. Students involved in the manufacturing process must have a deep understanding of these regulations to ensure that the packaging meets all the necessary requirements. This includes factors such as sterility maintenance, label accuracy, and tamper-evident features.

Secondly, the packaging must be designed to protect the medical device from damage during transit and storage. Students should consider the fragility of the device and select appropriate materials and cushioning techniques to safeguard it. Additionally, they should take into account the environmental factors that the device may be exposed to, such as temperature, humidity, and pressure, and design the packaging accordingly.

Furthermore, usability and user-friendliness should not be overlooked. Medical devices are often used by healthcare professionals in critical situations, and the packaging should facilitate easy and quick access to the device. Students can explore various packaging designs that allow for efficient and ergonomic use, such as peelable pouches, blister packs, or sterile trays.

Finally, sustainability is a growing concern in the field of manufacturing engineering. Students should incorporate eco-friendly packaging materials and designs whenever possible, reducing waste and environmental impact. This could include the use of recyclable materials, minimizing excess packaging, and exploring innovative solutions like biodegradable or compostable materials.

In conclusion, packaging considerations for medical devices are of utmost importance in the field of manufacturing engineering. Students must be aware of regulatory requirements, design packaging that ensures the safety and protection of the device, prioritize usability, and incorporate sustainable practices. By paying attention to these crucial factors, students can contribute to the development of efficient, reliable, and environmentally conscious packaging solutions for medical devices.

Sterilization Methods and Validation

In the realm of medical device manufacturing, ensuring the safety and efficacy of products is of paramount importance. One critical aspect of this process is the sterilization of medical devices, which involves the elimination of all viable microorganisms that could potentially cause harm or infection. This subchapter will explore various sterilization methods employed in the field and shed light on the validation processes necessary to ensure their effectiveness.

Sterilization methods can be broadly classified into physical and chemical methods. Physical methods include heat, radiation, and filtration, while chemical methods involve the use of sterilizing agents such as ethylene oxide and hydrogen peroxide. Each method has its advantages and limitations, and it is crucial for manufacturing engineers to understand their principles and applications.

Heat sterilization, commonly known as autoclaving, is widely used due to its effectiveness and affordability. It works by subjecting medical devices to high temperatures and pressures, effectively killing microorganisms. Radiation sterilization, on the other hand, utilizes ionizing radiation to disrupt the DNA of microorganisms, rendering them incapable of reproduction. Filtration sterilization involves passing a liquid or gas through a membrane with a defined pore size, trapping microorganisms and preventing their passage.

While these sterilization methods are effective, it is crucial to validate their efficacy to ensure that medical devices are truly sterilized. Validation involves a series of tests and experiments to determine if a sterilization process consistently achieves the desired sterility assurance level (SAL). These tests evaluate the resistance of microorganisms to the sterilization method, the distribution of sterilizing agents, and the stability of the device during the sterilization process.

Manufacturing engineering students must understand the importance of validation and the regulatory requirements associated with it. They need to be familiar with relevant standards and guidelines, such as ISO 11135 for ethylene oxide sterilization and ISO 11137 for radiation sterilization. They must also be aware of validation challenges, such as the impact of device design on sterilization efficacy, and develop strategies to overcome these challenges.

In conclusion, sterilization methods and validation are crucial aspects of manufacturing medical devices. Students in the field of manufacturing engineering must be well-versed in the principles and applications of different sterilization methods, as well as the validation processes necessary to ensure their effectiveness. By understanding these concepts, students can contribute to the development and production of safe and reliable medical devices that improve patient outcomes.

Shelf Life and Packaging Integrity Testing

In the world of medical devices, ensuring the safety and efficacy of products is of utmost importance. This is where shelf life and packaging integrity testing come into play. In this subchapter, we will delve into the significance of these tests and their role in the manufacturing engineering of medical devices.

Shelf life testing is the process of determining the length of time that a product can be stored under specified conditions while maintaining its quality and effectiveness. It involves subjecting the medical devices to accelerated aging conditions, simulating the real-life environment they may encounter during storage and transportation. By doing so, manufacturers can assess the product's stability, performance, and reliability over time.

Packaging integrity testing focuses on ensuring that the packaging of medical devices remains intact throughout its shelf life. Packaging plays a vital role in safeguarding the product from external factors such as moisture, light, and physical damage. Therefore, it is crucial to evaluate the integrity of the packaging, as any compromise can lead to contamination, sterility issues, or damage to the device itself.

Various testing methods are employed to assess packaging integrity, such as dye penetration, bubble emission, and vacuum decay testing. These tests help identify potential leaks or defects in the packaging, allowing manufacturers to take corrective actions before the product reaches the market.

For students pursuing a career in manufacturing engineering, understanding shelf life and packaging integrity testing is of great significance. It enables them to contribute to the development of safe and reliable medical devices. By incorporating these tests into the design and manufacturing process, students can ensure that the devices they create meet the highest quality standards and comply with regulatory requirements.

Additionally, students should familiarize themselves with the relevant regulations and standards governing shelf life and packaging integrity testing. Organizations like the Food and Drug Administration (FDA) and International Organization for Standardization (ISO) have established guidelines and requirements that manufacturers must adhere to. By having a thorough understanding of these regulations, students can ensure compliance and contribute to the overall success of their manufacturing projects.

In conclusion, shelf life and packaging integrity testing are essential aspects of manufacturing engineering in the medical device industry. These tests help assess the stability, performance, and reliability of products over time and ensure the integrity of their packaging. By understanding and implementing these tests, students can contribute to the development of safe and effective medical devices that meet the highest quality standards.

Chapter 9: Post-Market Surveillance and Risk Management

Overview of Post-Market Surveillance

Post-market surveillance is a crucial aspect of the medical device industry that ensures the safety and effectiveness of medical devices after they have been approved for market release. It involves the systematic collection, analysis, and interpretation of data related to the performance and safety of medical devices in real-world clinical settings. This subchapter aims to provide students in the field of manufacturing engineering with an overview of post-market surveillance and its significance in the development and maintenance of medical devices.

Post-market surveillance plays a vital role in monitoring the performance of medical devices once they enter the market. It helps identify any unexpected adverse events, malfunctions, or other safety concerns that may not have been detected during the pre-market testing phase. By continuously monitoring and evaluating the performance of medical devices, manufacturers can take prompt action to address any potential issues and ensure patient safety.

The subchapter will introduce students to the key components of post-market surveillance, including the importance of adverse event reporting, complaint handling, and feedback from healthcare professionals and patients. It will delve into the regulatory requirements surrounding post-market surveillance, emphasizing the need for compliance with applicable standards and regulations set forth by regulatory bodies such as the Food and Drug Administration (FDA) in the United States.

Furthermore, the subchapter will discuss the role of manufacturing engineers in post-market surveillance. Students will learn how manufacturing engineers contribute to the collection and analysis of post-market data, as well as their involvement in implementing corrective and preventive actions based on the findings. It will highlight the importance of collaboration between manufacturing engineers, regulatory affairs professionals, and other stakeholders to ensure effective post-market surveillance strategies.

Throughout the subchapter, real-world examples and case studies will be provided to illustrate the significance of post-market surveillance in identifying and addressing safety concerns. These examples will help students understand the potential impact of post-market surveillance on patient outcomes and the overall reputation of medical device manufacturers.

By the end of this subchapter, students will have a comprehensive understanding of the importance of post-market surveillance in the field of manufacturing engineering. They will be equipped with the knowledge and skills necessary to actively contribute to the development and maintenance of safe and effective medical devices throughout their careers in the industry.

Adverse Event Reporting and Corrective Actions

In the field of manufacturing engineering, particularly in the medical devices industry, the utmost priority is ensuring the safety and effectiveness of the products being developed. Adverse event reporting and corrective actions play a crucial role in this process. This subchapter aims to shed light on the significance of these practices and the role they play in maintaining quality standards.

When it comes to medical devices, adverse events refer to any untoward incident or undesirable effect associated with the use of a product. These events can range from minor inconveniences to serious injuries or even fatalities. As manufacturing engineering students, it is essential to understand the importance of reporting adverse events promptly and accurately.

Adverse event reporting serves multiple purposes. Firstly, it helps manufacturers identify potential issues with their products, allowing them to take immediate action to rectify the problem. This ensures that the devices meet the required safety and performance standards. Secondly, it contributes to the overall knowledge base, allowing researchers and regulatory bodies to gain a comprehensive understanding of the risks associated with specific medical devices. This knowledge can then be used to develop better practices and regulations to enhance patient safety.

Corrective actions are the subsequent steps taken by manufacturers to address the reported adverse events. These actions can include product recalls, design modifications, manufacturing process improvements, or even changes in labeling and instructions for use. As students of manufacturing engineering, it is vital to understand the significance of these corrective actions in maintaining the integrity of medical devices.

Furthermore, this subchapter will delve into the regulatory framework surrounding adverse event reporting and corrective actions. Students will gain insights into the various regulatory bodies involved, such as the Food and Drug Administration (FDA) in the United States, and the specific guidelines they provide for manufacturers to follow. Understanding these regulations is crucial for students aspiring to enter the field of manufacturing engineering, as compliance is essential for ensuring the safety and effectiveness of medical devices.

In conclusion, adverse event reporting and corrective actions are integral components of manufacturing engineering in the medical devices industry. By studying and implementing these practices, students can contribute to the development of safer and more effective medical devices. This subchapter aims to provide students with a comprehensive understanding of the importance of adverse event reporting, the subsequent corrective actions, and the regulatory framework surrounding these practices.

Risk Management in the Post-Market Phase

As students in the field of Manufacturing Engineering, it is crucial to understand the importance of risk management in the post-market phase of medical device development. This subchapter will delve into the key principles and practices that must be followed to ensure the safety and effectiveness of medical devices once they are on the market.

The post-market phase refers to the period after a medical device has been approved and made available for use. During this phase, manufacturers have an ongoing responsibility to monitor the device's performance, identify any potential risks or issues, and take appropriate actions to mitigate them. This is crucial for maintaining patient safety and ensuring that the device continues to meet its intended purpose.

One of the primary aspects of post-market risk management is vigilance. Manufacturers must establish systems and processes to collect and evaluate data on the device's performance in real-world settings. This includes monitoring adverse events, conducting post-market surveillance studies, and engaging with healthcare professionals and patients to gather feedback.

Additionally, manufacturers should have a robust complaint handling system in place to address any concerns or issues raised by users of the device. This system should include clear procedures for investigating complaints, documenting findings, and implementing corrective and preventive actions as necessary.

Risk management in the post-market phase also involves conducting periodic safety and performance reviews. Manufacturers must establish a process for systematically reviewing and analyzing data collected during the post-market phase to identify any potential safety issues or performance concerns. This information can then be used to inform decision-making and take appropriate actions, such as issuing safety alerts, updating labeling or instructions for use, or even initiating a product recall if necessary.

Furthermore, manufacturers should actively engage in post-market surveillance activities, such as participating in registries or post-approval studies. These initiatives allow for the collection of long-term data on the device's performance and can help identify any trends or patterns that may indicate potential risks or areas for improvement.

In conclusion, risk management in the post-market phase is a critical aspect of medical device development. As students in the field of Manufacturing Engineering, it is essential to understand the principles and practices involved in ensuring the safety and effectiveness of medical devices once they are on the market. By implementing robust systems for vigilance, complaint handling, safety and performance reviews, and post-market surveillance, manufacturers can fulfill their ongoing responsibilities and contribute to the overall improvement of patient care.

Chapter 10: Future Trends and Innovations in Medical Device Manufacturing

Advances in Biomaterials for Medical Devices

In recent years, the field of medical device manufacturing engineering has witnessed significant advancements in the development of biomaterials. These materials have revolutionized the design and functionality of medical devices, offering exciting possibilities for improving patient care and treatment outcomes. This subchapter will explore the latest breakthroughs in biomaterials for medical devices, providing valuable insights for students in the field of manufacturing engineering.

Biomaterials, as the name suggests, are materials that interact with biological systems. They are designed to be biocompatible, meaning they do not cause any harm or adverse reactions when in contact with living tissues. The development of biomaterials has opened up new avenues in medical device design, allowing for the creation of devices that seamlessly integrate with the human body.

One significant advance in biomaterials is the use of biodegradable materials. These materials have the ability to degrade over time, eliminating the need for surgical removal of medical devices after they have served their purpose. Biodegradable biomaterials are particularly beneficial in applications such as drug delivery systems, where the device gradually releases medication while simultaneously degrading in the body.

Another exciting development is the integration of smart materials into medical devices. Smart materials have the ability to respond to external stimuli, such as temperature, pH, or mechanical forces. By incorporating these materials into medical devices, engineers can create devices that can adapt and respond to the specific needs of each patient. For example, smart materials can enable the controlled release of medication based on the patient's current condition, optimizing treatment effectiveness.

Advancements in biomaterials have also led to the development of bioactive materials. These materials have the ability to stimulate specific cellular responses, promoting tissue growth and regeneration. By utilizing bioactive materials in medical devices, engineers can create implants that integrate seamlessly with surrounding tissues, enhancing the healing process and reducing the risk of complications.

Furthermore, the emergence of nanotechnology has opened up new frontiers in biomaterials research. Nanomaterials, with their unique properties at the nanoscale, offer exciting possibilities for medical device design. For instance, nanoparticles can be used to enhance the mechanical properties of biomaterials, improving their strength and durability. Additionally, nanotechnology enables precise control over the size, shape, and surface properties of biomaterials, enhancing their biocompatibility and functionality.

In conclusion, advances in biomaterials have revolutionized the field of medical device manufacturing engineering. The development of biodegradable, smart, bioactive, and nanomaterials has opened up new possibilities for creating innovative and patient-centric medical devices. As students in the field of manufacturing engineering, understanding these advancements in biomaterials is crucial for designing and developing cutting-edge medical devices that can enhance patient care and treatment outcomes.

Integration of Artificial Intelligence and Internet of Things (IoT) in Medical Device Manufacturing

In recent years, the integration of artificial intelligence (AI) and Internet of Things (IoT) technologies has revolutionized various industries, including medical device manufacturing. As students pursuing a career in manufacturing engineering, it is crucial to understand the implications and potential benefits of this integration in the context of medical device production.

The integration of AI and IoT in medical device manufacturing has brought forth numerous advancements and improvements. AI algorithms and machine learning techniques have made it possible to analyze large amounts of data collected through IoT devices, enabling manufacturers to make informed decisions and optimize their processes. This data-driven approach has significantly enhanced the efficiency, accuracy, and quality of medical device manufacturing.

One of the key benefits of integrating AI and IoT in medical device manufacturing is predictive maintenance. IoT devices embedded in the manufacturing equipment collect real-time data on performance, temperature, and other relevant parameters. AI algorithms then analyze this data to predict when maintenance or repairs may be required, preventing equipment failures and minimizing downtime. This proactive approach not only ensures uninterrupted production but also reduces costs associated with unexpected breakdowns.

Another area where AI and IoT integration has made a significant impact is in quality control. IoT sensors placed at different stages of the manufacturing process can monitor various parameters, such as temperature, pressure, and vibration. AI algorithms can then analyze this data in real-time, identifying any deviations from the desired specifications. This enables manufacturers to detect and rectify potential defects early on, ensuring that only high-quality devices reach the market.

Moreover, the integration of AI and IoT has also paved the way for personalized medicine. IoT-enabled medical devices can collect patient-specific data, such as vital signs, activity levels, and medication adherence. AI algorithms can then analyze this data to provide personalized treatment recommendations and interventions, improving patient outcomes. This combination of AI and IoT has the potential to revolutionize healthcare, enabling more accurate diagnoses, personalized treatments, and better patient care.

As students in the field of manufacturing engineering, it is essential to stay informed and up-to-date with the latest technological advancements. The integration of AI and IoT in medical device manufacturing is an exciting and rapidly evolving field with immense potential. By understanding the implications and benefits of this integration, you can contribute to the development and advancement of medical devices that improve the lives of patients worldwide.

In conclusion, the integration of AI and IoT in medical device manufacturing has brought about significant advancements in efficiency, quality control, predictive maintenance, and personalized medicine. As students in the field of manufacturing engineering, it is crucial to embrace these technologies and explore their potential applications in the production of medical devices. By doing so, you can contribute to the advancement of healthcare and make a lasting impact on the industry.

Personalized Medicine and Customized Medical Devices

In recent years, advancements in technology have revolutionized the healthcare industry, particularly in the field of personalized medicine and customized medical devices. This subchapter aims to introduce students in the field of manufacturing engineering to the exciting possibilities and challenges associated with this emerging trend.

Personalized medicine is a groundbreaking approach that tailors medical treatments to individual patients based on their genetic makeup, lifestyle, and other unique characteristics. By analyzing a person's genomic profile, doctors can determine the most effective treatments and therapies, minimizing trial and error and optimizing patient outcomes. This shift from a one-size-fits-all approach to a more personalized model has the potential to revolutionize healthcare by improving patient care and reducing healthcare costs.

One critical aspect of personalized medicine is the development of customized medical devices. These devices are designed to fit perfectly with an individual's unique anatomy, ensuring optimal comfort, functionality, and effectiveness. From prosthetic limbs to orthopedic implants, 3D printing and other advanced manufacturing technologies have opened up new avenues for creating personalized medical devices.

Manufacturing engineering students play a vital role in the design, development, and production of these customized medical devices. By combining their knowledge of engineering principles with an understanding of medical requirements, students can contribute to the creation of innovative solutions that address specific patient needs.

This subchapter will provide students with insights into the design considerations, materials selection, and manufacturing techniques involved in the production of personalized medical devices.

Additionally, students will learn about the regulatory and ethical aspects associated with personalized medicine and customized medical devices. As these devices are tailored to individual patients, ensuring their safety and efficacy becomes even more crucial. By understanding the regulatory landscape and ethical considerations, manufacturing engineering students can contribute to the development of compliant and responsible solutions.

Personalized medicine and customized medical devices represent the future of healthcare. By embracing this trend, students in manufacturing engineering can become catalysts for change, driving innovation and improving patient outcomes. This subchapter aims to equip students with the knowledge and tools necessary to contribute to this exciting field and make a positive impact on the lives of millions.

Chapter 11: Career Opportunities and Professional Development in Medical Device Manufacturing Engineering

Job Roles and Responsibilities in Medical Device Manufacturing

In the world of manufacturing engineering, the medical device industry holds a unique and critical position. The development and production of medical devices require a high level of precision, quality control, and adherence to strict regulations. As students in the field of manufacturing engineering, it is crucial to understand the various job roles and responsibilities within the medical device manufacturing sector.

1. Design Engineers: Design engineers play a vital role in medical device manufacturing. They are responsible for conceptualizing, designing, and developing new medical devices or improving existing ones. Their work involves understanding user needs, conducting research, creating prototypes, and collaborating with other engineering disciplines to ensure the safety, effectiveness, and manufacturability of the device.

2. Quality Assurance Engineers: Quality assurance engineers are responsible for ensuring that all medical devices meet regulatory standards and specifications. They develop and implement quality control processes, conduct inspections, and perform tests to validate the device's functionality and reliability. Their role is critical to ensuring the safety and efficacy of medical devices.

3. **Manufacturing Engineers:** Manufacturing engineers are involved in the production process of medical devices. They work closely with design engineers to translate product designs into manufacturing processes. Their responsibilities include selecting appropriate materials, designing production lines, optimizing manufacturing operations, and ensuring efficient and cost-effective production.

4. **Regulatory Affairs Specialists:** Regulatory affairs specialists are responsible for navigating the complex landscape of medical device regulations. They ensure that all devices comply with applicable laws and regulations, such as the Food and Drug Administration (FDA) requirements. Their role involves preparing and submitting documentation, coordinating with regulatory agencies, and keeping abreast of the latest regulatory changes.

5. **Process Validation Engineers:** Process validation engineers focus on validating the manufacturing processes used to produce medical devices. They design experiments, analyze data, and ensure that the processes consistently meet quality standards. Their role is instrumental in ensuring the reliability and repeatability of the manufacturing processes.

6. **Project Managers:** Project managers oversee the entire manufacturing process, ensuring that projects are completed within budget, on time, and meet quality requirements. They coordinate between different teams, manage resources, and ensure effective communication throughout the project lifecycle.

Understanding the various job roles and responsibilities in medical device manufacturing provides students in the field of manufacturing engineering with valuable insights into the industry. It highlights the interdisciplinary nature of the field and the importance of collaboration and adherence to regulatory standards. By familiarizing themselves with these job roles, students can better prepare themselves for a successful career in the challenging and rewarding field of medical device manufacturing.

Continuing Education and Professional Certifications

In the rapidly evolving field of manufacturing engineering, it is crucial for students to understand the significance of continuing education and professional certifications. As technology advances and industries become more competitive, staying current and upgrading skills is essential to thriving in the field of medical device manufacturing. This subchapter aims to shed light on the importance of continuous learning and the benefits of obtaining professional certifications.

Continuing education offers students the opportunity to enhance their knowledge and skills beyond the classroom. It provides a platform for staying up-to-date with the latest advancements, industry trends, and regulatory requirements in medical device manufacturing. By attending workshops, conferences, and seminars, students can gain insights from industry experts, network with professionals, and learn about emerging technologies. This exposure can be instrumental in broadening their perspective and understanding the challenges and opportunities that lie ahead.

Professional certifications are a testament to an individual's commitment to excellence and their expertise in a specific area of manufacturing engineering. These certifications validate the knowledge and skills acquired through formal education and practical experience. They demonstrate to potential employers that students possess the necessary competencies to excel in the field. In the context of medical device manufacturing, certifications such as Certified Medical Device Professional (CMDP) or Certified Manufacturing Engineer (CMfgE) can significantly boost career prospects and open doors to exciting opportunities.

Obtaining professional certifications not only enhances employability but also instills confidence in students. It equips them with a competitive edge, allowing them to stand out from the crowd. Certifications demonstrate a dedication to personal and professional growth, indicating to employers that the candidate is committed to staying current in their field. This commitment to continuous learning is highly valued by employers, as it aligns with the dynamic and ever-evolving nature of the medical device manufacturing industry.

Furthermore, professional certifications can lead to higher earning potential. Studies consistently show that professionals with certifications earn more than their non-certified counterparts. By investing in their education and obtaining relevant certifications, students can position themselves for better salary negotiations and career advancement.

In conclusion, continuing education and professional certifications are invaluable assets for students pursuing a career in manufacturing engineering, particularly in the medical device industry. By embracing lifelong learning and obtaining relevant certifications, students can stay ahead of the curve, demonstrate their expertise, and maximize their career opportunities. The field of medical device manufacturing is dynamic and demands continuous improvement. By actively engaging in continuing education and pursuing professional certifications, students can unlock their full potential and contribute to the advancement of this vital industry.

Networking and Industry Engagement for Career Advancement

In today's competitive job market, it is not enough to simply have a degree in manufacturing engineering. To truly excel in your career and stand out from the crowd, it is crucial to develop a strong network and engage with industry professionals. Networking and industry engagement are essential tools for career advancement in the field of manufacturing engineering.

Networking allows you to build relationships, gain insights, and discover new opportunities. By connecting with professionals in the industry, you can learn from their experiences, seek guidance, and stay updated on the latest trends and technologies. Attending conferences, seminars, and industry events provides a platform to meet like-minded individuals and establish meaningful connections. By actively participating in these events, you can expand your network and potentially find mentors who can guide you throughout your career journey.

In addition to networking, industry engagement plays a vital role in career advancement. Engaging with the industry allows you to gain practical experience and knowledge that cannot be acquired solely through academic studies. Internships, co-op programs, and industry projects provide hands-on experience and the opportunity to work on real-world manufacturing engineering challenges. This practical exposure not only enhances your skills but also makes you more attractive to potential employers.

Furthermore, industry engagement can open doors to potential job opportunities. Many companies prefer to hire candidates with prior industry experience, and by actively engaging with the industry, you increase your chances of securing a job after graduation. Additionally, industry professionals often have valuable insights into the skills and expertise that are in high demand. By staying engaged with the industry, you can align your education and skillset with the current needs of the manufacturing engineering field, making you a desirable candidate for future employment.

To effectively network and engage with the industry, it is important to develop strong communication and interpersonal skills. Building relationships requires active listening, effective communication, and the ability to collaborate with others. Developing these skills will not only benefit your networking efforts but also enhance your overall professional growth.

In conclusion, networking and industry engagement are indispensable for career advancement in the field of manufacturing engineering. By actively participating in networking events, seeking industry engagement opportunities, and developing strong communication skills, you can build a strong professional network, gain practical experience, and increase your chances of securing a fulfilling career in manufacturing engineering. Embrace these tools, and open doors to endless possibilities for your future success in the industry.

Chapter 12: Conclusion and Reflections on the Student's Journey in Medical Device Manufacturing Engineering

Congratulations, dear students, on reaching the final chapter of "Designing and Developing Medical Devices: A Student's Journey in Manufacturing Engineering." Throughout this book, we have embarked on an incredible journey together, exploring the fascinating world of medical device manufacturing engineering. Now, as we conclude our exploration, it's time to reflect on the invaluable lessons learned and the transformative experiences gained.

In this concluding chapter, we will recap the key highlights of our journey, emphasizing the significance of each step taken. We will delve into the various challenges faced and the learning opportunities they presented. Moreover, we will discuss the importance of critical thinking, innovation, and collaboration in the field of manufacturing engineering.

Throughout the book, we have covered a wide range of topics, starting with the fundamental principles of medical device manufacturing engineering. We explored the design process, materials selection, and the intricacies of manufacturing techniques. We dived into the realm of quality control, regulatory compliance, and risk management. Each chapter has provided you with a comprehensive understanding of the multifaceted nature of this field.

As students of manufacturing engineering, you have been introduced to the latest technological advancements that are shaping the industry. From additive manufacturing to automation and robotics, we have explored how these innovations are revolutionizing medical device manufacturing. We have also discussed the ethical considerations and sustainability aspects that should underpin your work as future engineers.

It is essential to note that your journey does not end with the completion of this book. In fact, it is only the beginning. As you step into the professional world, take these reflections with you. Embrace the challenges that lie ahead and never stop seeking knowledge and self-improvement. Remember that the field of manufacturing engineering is continually evolving, and you, as the next generation of engineers, have a crucial role to play in its advancement.

Lastly, I urge you to cultivate a passion for innovation and a commitment to improving patient care through your work. Medical device manufacturing engineering is not just about machines and processes; it is about making a difference in people's lives. Your dedication to excellence and your unwavering pursuit of innovation can lead to breakthroughs that transform healthcare and save countless lives.

As we conclude our journey together, I would like to express my sincere gratitude for joining me on this adventure. I hope that "Designing and Developing Medical Devices: A Student's Journey in Manufacturing Engineering" has equipped you with the knowledge, skills, and inspiration to succeed in this exciting field. Remember that your journey as a manufacturing engineer has just begun, and the possibilities are boundless.

Good luck, students, as you embark on your own journeys in medical device manufacturing engineering. Embrace the challenges, seize the opportunities, and make a lasting impact on the world.

www.ingramcontent.com/pod-product-compliance
Lightning Source LLC
LaVergne TN
LVHW052000060526
838201LV00059B/3751